Chomp

A College Cookbook

Written by real college moms

Lisa Botto &

Tammy Fischetti

D1364748

Introduction

Let's be honest, college students do not have time to sleep, let alone feed themselves. They need to learn how to make healthy, quick, and flavorful meals that are nutritious for a growing brain. Junk food leaves them feeling energized for that moment, but the crash has them tired and unsatisfied. By the end of the first semester of college, they are probably sick of the same lukewarm food in the dining halls. Therefore, it is important for college students to learn how to cook for themselves, plan ahead, and take charge of their own eating habits.

Our Chomp College Cooking Book comes with over 80 nutritious recipes ideal for the college students' busy schedule. The recipes are simple, cost effective, and most of all require little prep work. Each recipe comes with illustration and our Botto-Fischetti cooking tips for your guidance and new ideas. Plus, cooking at home saves money, which equals more entertainment with friends, more shopping, or simply saving money for the future (which is always a great thing to do)!

We hope this book will guide the college students on their academic journey with nutritional recipes to help along the way!

TABLE OF CONTENTS

KITCHEN STAPLES

If you stock up on any of these kitchen staples, it will keep you from having to make repeated trips to the grocery store and save you time in preparing meals.

Here are the essentials you will need:

Pantry:
- Flour: white or whole wheat flour
- Sugar: white, brown sugar, or coconut sugar, honey
- Baking Powder: baking soda, cornstarch
- Olive Oil: vegetable oil, peanut oil
- Vinegar: red wine vinegar, rice wine vinegar, balsamic vinegar
- Pasta Noodles: penne, linguine, fettuccini, rigatoni, bowties, orzo, angel hair
- Grains: white, brown rice, barley, quinoa, oats, couscous
- Nuts and Seeds: sunflower seeds, almonds, cashews, peanuts, chia seeds, flax seeds
- Peanut Butter: almond butter
- Onions: red or yellow onion
- Garlic
- Can Beans: kidney, garbanzo, black beans, pinto, chili beans
- Broth: chicken, beef, or vegetable broth
- Potatoes: sweet potatoes, baked potato, red potato
- Tomato Sauce: marinara sauce, stewed tomatoes, tomato paste

Appliances:
- Prep Bowls: mixing bowls

- Blender: food processor, mixer
- Pots and Frying pans: saucepan, sauté pan, grill pan, griddle, cast iron
- Baking sheet: oven mitts
- Aluminum Foil: saran wrap, parchment paper
- Utensils: forks, knives, spoons, spatula, whisk, can opener, peeler, grater, tongs, measuring spoons, measuring cups, timer, colander
- Cutting Board: kitchen towels

Spices:
- Salt: kosher, sea salt
- Pepper: black pepper, white pepper
- Dried herbs: parsley, basil, bay leaves, oregano, garlic powder, onion, cinnamon, chili, cumin powder, cayenne pepper, red pepper flakes, vanilla extract

Refrigerated Items:
- Butter: vegan butter, cooking spray
- Eggs: white, or brown eggs
- Milk: almond milk
- Cheese: cheddar, feta, mozzarella, parmesan, goat
- Dijon mustard: yellow, brown mustard
- Ketchup: barbeque sauce, hot sauce, soy sauce
- Mayonnaise: vegan mayonnaise
- Jelly
- Lemon Juice: lime juice

BREAKFAST

INDIVIDUAL EGG FRITTATAS IN A MUFFIN PAN

- 8 large eggs
- 1 zucchini, finely chopped
- 1 red bell pepper, chopped
- ½ yellow onion, diced
- 3-4 slices of turkey or any other lunch meat (optional)
- ½ cup spinach
- ½ teaspoon salt
- ½ teaspoon black pepper
- 1 tablespoon of milk (or water)
- 1 tablespoon fresh or dry parsley
- ½ cup of feta, cheddar or mozzarella cheese
- Cooking spray (muffin pan)

Preheat oven to 350°F degrees. Spray muffin pan with cooking spray. Crack eggs into a bowl, add rest of ingredients, and whisk well. Using a ladle pour egg mixture into each muffin cup until filled halfway. Bake at 350°F for 20-25 minutes until firm and lightly browned.

Botto-Fischetti Tip: *You can add any vegetable or cheese. Add a kick of tabasco sauce for heat. Enjoy eating them anytime of the day! Great snack between classes.*

WHOLE WHEAT CINNAMON FRENCH TOAST

- 2-4 slices of whole wheat bread
- 2 eggs, whipped
- 1 tablespoon of water
- 1 tablespoon of vanilla
- ½ teaspoon of cinnamon
- 1 cup of sliced strawberries
- ½ tablespoon of confectioner's sugar
- Maple syrup or honey
- Cool whip
- Grill pan & Cooking spray

Spray cooking spray on your grill pan and heat to medium high heat.

In a large bowl, crack 2 eggs with 1 tablespoon of water. Add vanilla and cinnamon to your egg mixture and mix well. Dip your bread in the egg mixture and add to the grill pan.

Cook for about 2 minutes until the first side of the French toast is golden brown. Gently flip to the other side and cook for another 2 minutes.

Transfer to a plate and add sliced strawberries on one side of your French toast and cool whip on the other side. Top with more strawberries, sprinkle confectioner's sugar all over the top and drizzle syrup or honey.

Botto-Fischetti Tip: *Serve with scrambled eggs and fruit!*

KALE AND STRAWBERRY SMOOTHIES

- 1½ cup chopped kale
- ½ cup Greek yogurt (plain or flavored)
- ½ cup milk or water
- ½ cup strawberries (any berries)
- 1 tablespoon honey
- 1 teaspoon cinnamon
- 6-7 ice cubes
- Blender

Put all ingredients in the blender and mix well until smooth.

Botto-Fischetti Tip: *You can always add protein powder to the smoothie and peanut butter. Coconut water and frozen berries works great as well.*

BLUEBERRY AND OATS SMOOTHIE

- ½ cup fresh blueberries
- ½ cup rolled oats
- 1 ripe banana
- 1 cup spinach
- ½ teaspoon fresh ginger
- 1 cup almond milk (any milk)
- Dash of cinnamon
- 1 cup ice cubes

Put all ingredients in a blender. Blend away!

Botto-Fischetti Tip: *Coconut water can work as well.*

GRANOLA AND FLAX SEED BREAKFAST PARFAIT

- ⅓ cup fresh raspberries
- ⅓ cup fresh blackberries
- ⅓ cup granola
- ½ teaspoon honey
- ½ teaspoon flax seeds
- ½ cup nonfat vanilla yogurt
- Sprinkle cinnamon

Put all ingredients in a bowl or glass jar. Sprinkle cinnamon over the top. Keep refrigerated until ready to eat.

Botto-Fischetti Tip: *You can use any fruit you like.*

CHOCOLATE CHIP BUTTERMILK PANCAKES

- 2 cups all-purpose flour
- ¼ cup sugar
- ½ teaspoon salt
- 1 teaspoon baking soda
- 2 large eggs
- 2½ cups buttermilk
- ¼ cup melted butter or vegetable oil
- Chocolate chips
- Additional butter for cooking

Combine flour, sugar, salt and baking soda together in large bowl.

In separate bowl mix eggs, buttermilk and melted butter until well combined. Gently fold into flour mixture, combining but do not over mix, will have pea-sized lumps.

Preheat nonstick pan or griddle to medium, if desired melt a little butter in bottom (will help pancakes brown and be a bit crispier) ladle 3-4 tablespoons batter for each pancake and sprinkle chocolate chips evenly over. Cook until golden brown and bubbles on top begin to burst. Flip over and cook second side until browned (will take less time).

Serve immediately with butter, syrup, whipping cream or topping of your choice.

PLAIN WAFFLES

- 2 large eggs
- 1¾ cups milk (whole, skim or nonfat)
- ½ cup melted butter or vegetable oil
- 2 tablespoons sugar
- 1 teaspoon vanilla extract
- 2 cups all-purpose flour
- 4 teaspoons baking powder
- ½ teaspoon salt
- Waffle iron

In large bowl beat eggs until light and fluffy, add milk, butter or oil, sugar and vanilla extract mixing until thoroughly combined.

In a separate bowl combine flour, baking powder and salt. Add dry ingredients to liquid mixture and mix until smooth. Let rest 15 minutes.

Lightly spray pre-heated waffle iron with non-cook spray and pour mix into a hot iron. Cook until golden brown and crispy.

Serve warm with butter, syrup, fruit, cream or whatever you like!

Botto-Fischetti Tip: *Use buttermilk instead of plain milk and replace ½ cup of flour with cornstarch for a lighter, crisper waffle.*

TOASTED AVOCADO SMASH

- 1-2 slices of toasted bread (any kind)
- 1 avocado, halved and pitted
- 1-2 cooked scrambled eggs
- 1-2 slices Canadian bacon (cooked) optional
- 1-2 Roma tomato, sliced
- ½ lemon squeezed
- ½-1 tablespoon of olive oil
- ½ teaspoon garlic powder
- ½ teaspoon salt
- Sprinkle red pepper flakes (optional)
- Sprinkle mozzarella cheese

In a bowl, mix avocado flesh, olive oil, salt, garlic powder, red pepper flakes and a squeeze of lemon. Mash all together with a fork. Taste for seasoning.

Toast your bread and spread avocado mixture over your toast, then add Canadian bacon, scrambled eggs and tomato slices. Add cheese for topping.

Botto-Fischetti Tip: *You can make a fried egg or poached instead of scrambled.*

21

BREAKFAST SIDES

BLUEBERRY AND STRAWBERRY JAM

- 1 pint of blueberries, rinsed
- 1 pint of strawberries, cut in half
- Zest of 1 lemon
- 1-2 tablespoon fresh lemon juice
- 4 sprigs of mint, chopped
- ⅓ cup of coconut sugar (or any sugar you like)

Use a medium size pot on medium to low heat and add all the berries, sugar, lemon zest, lemon juice and mint. Let it boil, and then reduce to low and use a masher to smash the fruit, to your desired smoothness.

Simmer on low for 15 minutes, stirring constantly until it thickens. Turn off the heat. Let it rest until it is completely cooled and put it in mason jars and keep refrigerated.

Botto-Fischetti Tip: *Use it on French toast, pancakes, crackers, or sandwiches. Make sure you clean your mason jar.*

HARD-BOILED EGGS

- 2 to 4 eggs
- Salt and Pepper

Place eggs in a medium size saucepan and fill with cold water to right above the eggs. Place on high heat and when the water boils, put a lid on the pot and turn off the heat. Let the eggs finish cooking for 10-12 minutes to get the perfect hard-boiled egg.

Drain and submerge in bowl of ice water to stop the cooking. Once cool, peel the shell of the egg and add salt and black pepper to taste.

Botto-Fischetti Tip: *Make it ahead of time; it will last in the fridge for a week. Great to snack on anytime during the day.*

SCRAMBLED EGGS

- 3-4 eggs
- 1 tablespoon heavy cream or milk
- ½ tablespoon unsalted butter (or olive oil)
- Sprinkle salt and black pepper
- 5 drops of Tabasco sauce optional (if you like it spicy add more drops)
- ¼ cup grated cheddar cheese

In a bowl crack eggs and add heavy cream, cheese, salt, pepper and tabasco. Whisk ingredients together. Heat a skillet over medium-low heat, add butter and milk, and pour the eggs into the skillet.

Using a spatula, stir eggs around and just keep stirring until the eggs are scrambled to your liking. Serve with toast and enjoy!

Botto-Fischetti Tip: *You can always add avocado, tomatoes, salsa and blueberry and strawberry jam. Or you can make this with egg whites as a healthier option.*

LUNCH

ROASTED VEGGIE GARDEN WRAPS

- 2-4 spinach wrap tortillas (or any kind)
- 1 small eggplant, sliced ½ inch thickness
- 1 small red bell pepper, sliced in big pieces
- 1 small red onion, sliced
- 1 small tub store bought hummus
- 1 8-ounce bottle oil packed sun-dried tomatoes, drained & chopped
- handful of fresh spinach leaves
- 1/4 cup olive oil
- 1 teaspoon salt
- 1 teaspoon black pepper
- sprinkle crumbled feta cheese

Preheat oven to 350°F degrees. In a bowl toss eggplant, red bell pepper and red onion in olive oil with salt and pepper. Place all the vegetables on a cooking sheet and bake for 30-45 minutes until golden brown and tender.

Heat up tortillas on ungreased skillet over medium heat for 5-7 seconds on each side. Spread hummus over the wrap and add roasted vegetables in the middle. Add cheese, spinach and sundried tomatoes on top of the cooked vegetables. Roll and tuck your tortilla wrap so it looks like a burrito.

Botto-Fischetti Tip: *You can always add protein, or any cheese you like in your wrap.*

PESTO, RICOTTA BRUSCHETTA

- 4-5 ripe plum tomatoes, chopped
- 1 6-ounce jar of pesto
- 1 15-ounce container ricotta cheese
- 3-4 garlic cloves, minced
- 1½ tablespoons extra virgin olive oil
- 1½ teaspoons balsamic vinegar
- 1 teaspoon salt
- ½ black pepper
- 6-8 basil leaves, thinly sliced
- 1 baguette French bread sliced
- ¼ cup olive oil for the baguette (French bread)

Preheat oven to 425°F degrees. Slice the baguette bread diagonally and brush the olive oil on each slice. Place on a baking sheet and bake the baguettes in the oven on the top rack until lightly golden brown, about 5-6 minutes.

In a medium bowl toss tomato, garlic, salt, pepper, basil, olive oil and balsamic vinegar together, and let marinate for 1-2 hours in the refrigerator. Taste for seasoning.

Once the baguettes are slightly cooled, spread a layer of pesto on each slice of the baguette, then add a light layer of ricotta cheese on top of the pesto, and finally spoon the tomato mixture on top of that.

<u>Botto-Fischetti Tip:</u> *You can make this also without pesto.*

TURKEY HUMMUS & SWISS CHEESE SANDWICH

- 2 slices whole wheat bread
- 3-4 slices turkey deli lunch meat
- 2-3 tablespoons pre-made hummus
- 2-4 slices of Swiss cheese
- 1 small tomato sliced
- Handful of spinach
- Sprinkle salt and pepper

Spread hummus on each slice of bread. Add turkey slices, Swiss cheese, tomato, spinach, salt and pepper to one side and top with another bread slice. Serve with chips or veggies.

AVOCADO SHRIMP SALAD

- 1 pound cooked shrimp, chopped
- 1½ avocados, cut in cubes
- ¼ cup red onion, finely chopped
- ½ cup halved cherry tomatoes
- 3-4 tablespoons fresh lime juice
- 3-4 tablespoons olive oil
- 1 teaspoon salt
- Sprinkle black pepper
- Lime zest
- Basil torn pieces

Mix all ingredients together in a bowl. Taste for seasoning. Keep refrigerated until ready to serve.

Botto-Fischetti Tip: *You can use salad size shrimp to make it easier. To add spice, add a drizzle of Sriracha to your shrimp.*

BROCCOLI, SUNFLOWER, AND GREEK YOGURT SALAD

- 4 cups broccoli florets (2 medium heads)
- ½ cup shredded carrots
- ½ cup chopped pecans
- ½ cup sunflower seeds
- ½ cup sliced red grapes
- ½ cup crumbled gorgonzola cheese
- ¼ cup diced red onion
- 2 large apples, chopped (any apples)

Dressing:
- ½ cup mayonnaise
- ¾ cup Greek yogurt (plain)
- 2 tablespoons lemon juice
- 1 tablespoon sugar
- ¼ teaspoon salt
- Sprinkle black pepper

In a medium size bowl toss all the salad ingredients together. Mix dressing in a separate bowl. Pour the dressing over the broccoli mixture. Taste for seasonings. Keep refrigerated until ready to serve.

ORGANIC BLACK BEAN TUNA WRAP

- 1 5-ounce can of organic tuna
- 1/4 cup organic black beans, drained and rinsed
- ¾ cup shredded lettuce
- ½ cup salsa
- ½ cup shredded Monterey jack cheese
- 2 large flour tortillas
- Hot sauce (optional)
- Sprinkle salt and pepper

In a bowl toss tuna, black beans, salsa, salt and pepper. Heat the tortillas in the microwave for 30 seconds. Spread the tuna mixture onto the center of the tortillas. Add lettuce and cheese and fold the edges up like a burrito and cut diagonally.

Botto-Fischetti Tip: *You can use any cheese you like. You can also add avocado or tomato.*

GRILLED CHICKEN BREAST & GREEN CHILI SANDWICHES

- 4 boneless skinless chicken breast halves
- 1 4-ounce can whole green chilies, drained
- 4 sliced cheese (jalapeno jack or cheddar)
- 4 hamburger buns
- Olive oil
- ½ teaspoon salt
- ¼ teaspoon black pepper
- Cooking spray

Warm a grill pan over medium heat. Slit green chilies to open flat. Brush olive oil over the chicken breast and season with salt and pepper. Cook 8 minutes on each side of the chicken, until no longer pink inside.

Remove chicken breast from the grill. Top each breast with a slice of cheese and a green chili. Toast buns on the grill until toasted. Serve with lettuce and tomato if desired. Chomp away!

ORGANIC PEANUT BUTTER & APRICOT JELLY WITH GREEN APPLES

- 2 slices organic wheat bread (or any kind)
- 2 tablespoons organic peanut butter
- 2 tablespoons organic apricot jelly (or any kind)
- 1 organic green apple, sliced thinly (or any kind)
- Sprinkle confectioner sugar for topping
- Cooking spray
- Panini Machine

Spray cooking spray on your Panini machine. Spread peanut butter on one side of the wheat bread. Add jelly on the other side and sliced apples. Grill the sandwich in the Panini machine and when it is done, sprinkle confectioners' sugar and cut in half and enjoy!

Botto-Fischetti Tip: *If you don't have a Panini machine, you can always use a grill.*

TURKEY & QUINOA BOWL

- 1 pound ground turkey
- 1 yellow onion, diced
- 2 garlic cloves, minced
- 1 8-ounce can water chestnuts, drained and chopped
- 1 16-ounce can tomato sauce
- 1 15-ounce can of kidney beans
- 1 cup of cooked quinoa
- 1-2 carrots, peeled and diced
- 1 green bell pepper, diced
- 3 tablespoons olive oil
- 2 teaspoons of salt
- 1 teaspoon of black pepper
- 1 tablespoon of Italian seasoning

In a large sauté pan, add olive oil on medium to high heat. Season ground turkey with salt and pepper. Cook, stirring and breaking up the meat with a wooden spoon for 5 minutes. Add onion, garlic, carrots, bell pepper, chestnuts and Italian seasoning.

Once the turkey mixture is cooked through, (no pink inside) add tomato sauce and kidney beans, bring to a boil, and then let it simmer on low for 20-25 minutes. Pour cooked quinoa over the top of turkey mixture and toss well. Check your seasoning. Divide into bowls and serve.

Botto-Fischetti Tip: *You can heat up tortillas and make tacos out of the mixture. Or skip the meat and make it a vegetarian dish! Also add cooked brown rice, spinach, kale and avocado at the very last minute, and then toss it all together.*

TURKEY LETTUCE WRAPS

- 1 tablespoon vegetable oil
- 1¼ pounds ground turkey (standard package size)
- 8-ounces mushrooms, finely chopped
- 2 large cloves garlic, minced
- 1 medium onion, finely diced
- ½ red pepper, finely chopped (optional)
- 1 tablespoon grated ginger
- ¼ cup hoisin sauce
- 2 tablespoons low sodium soy sauce
- 2 tablespoons rice wine vinegar
- 1-2 tablespoon Sriracha, depending on how spicy you like it
- 8-ounce can of water chestnuts, drained & chopped
- 1 large carrot, grated
- Chopped cilantro for garnish
- 1 head Iceberg or butter lettuce separated into leaves for serving

Heat oil in large pan over medium-high heat, crumble in turkey, add mushrooms and cook until turkey is cooked through. Add onion, garlic, bell pepper, ginger, and sauté until onions are translucent.

Add the hoisin sauce, soy sauce, vinegar, Sriracha, water chestnuts and carrots and stir until well combined and heated through. Garnish with cilantro and serve in lettuce cups.

Botto-Fischetti Tip: *Serve with sweet chili sauce such as "Mae Ploy".*

STUFFED AVOCADO WITH BULGUR & FETA CHEESE

- 1 avocado, split in half and remove the pit
- 1-2 tablespoons olive oil
- ⅓ cup bulgur (soaked in warm water and drained)
- ⅓ cup mushrooms
- 1 Roma tomato, finely chopped
- ⅓ cup toasted chopped almonds
- ⅓ cup sunflower seeds, unsalted
- ½ teaspoon salt
- ¼ teaspoon black pepper
- 1 lemon, juiced
- Handful fresh chopped parsley
- Sprinkle paprika
- Crumbled feta cheese

In a medium size sauté pan heat olive oil and sauté the mushrooms until golden brown. Chop the cooked mushrooms and put into a large bowl. Place bulgur in a small bowl, filled with warm water until the bulgur floats. Let it sit for a couple of minutes.

Drain the water from the bulgur and add to the bowl with the mushrooms. Add rest of the ingredients except paprika and feta and mix well. Fill avocado halves with mixture and finish off with feta cheese, paprika and drizzle olive oil over top. Season to taste.

Botto-Fischetti Tip: _You can add cooked baby shrimp to this dish as well._

CROCK POT TURKEY CHILI

- 1 pound ground turkey
- 1 large onion, chopped
- 2 medium garlic cloves, minced
- 2 tablespoons vegetable oil
- 1 teaspoon of honey
- 1 packet chili season mix (1.25ouce)
- 1 15-ounce can kidney beans, (rinsed and drained)
- 1 15-ounce can cannellini beans, (rinsed and drained)
- 1 15-ounce can pinto beans, (rinsed and drained)
- 1 15-ounce can black beans, (rinsed and drained)
- 2 14.5-ounce cans diced tomato with jalapenos
- 1½ cups of water
- 1 tablespoon chili powder
- 2 bay leaves
- 1 teaspoon salt
- 1 teaspoon black pepper
- Crock pot

Heat the oil in a large sauté pan over medium heat; add turkey, onion and garlic. Sauté for about 5-6 minutes until cooked through. Place turkey mixture in the crock- pot. Add the rest of the remaining ingredients to the crock- pot and stir to combine. Cover and cook the chili on high for 4 hours or on low for 8 hours. Top with your favorite chili fixings.

<u>Botto-Fischetti Tips</u>: *You can use beef or chicken for your protein, or you can make this a vegetarian dish. You can add sour cream, grated cheddar cheese, scallions, chips, or cornbread for your toppings! If you don't have a crockpot you can use a large pot over the stove and heat on low for about an hour. Taste for seasoning before serving.*

PITA & GOAT CHEESE BASIL PIZZA

- 1-2 whole-wheat pita bread
- ½ cup jar marinara sauce
- 2 tablespoon goat cheese, crumbled
- 2 tablespoons of grated cheddar cheese
- 3-4 mushrooms, sliced
- 1 tomato, sliced thinly
- sprinkle salt and black pepper
- 1-2 fresh basil leaves, torn in pieces
- Drizzle of olive oil (topping)
- 1 avocado sliced for topping (optional)
- Cooking spray

Preheat oven to 400°F degrees. Spray baking sheet with cooking spray and place pita bread on it. Spread the marinara sauce all over the pita bread. Add both cheeses, mushrooms, sliced tomato, salt and pepper. Bake for 8-10 minutes until cheese is melted.

When the pizza is done add avocado, torn basil, and drizzle olive oil on top.

Botto-Fischetti Tip: *Make ahead of time, and just bake when you are ready to eat.*

MOZZARELLA, TOMATO AND BASIL SALAD

- 2 large tomatoes, sliced about ¼ inch thick
- 8-ounce package pre-sliced fresh mozzarella cheese
- 4-5 fresh basil leaves, torn in pieces or (kept whole)
- 2 tablespoons extra virgin olive oil
- 1/2 tablespoon balsamic vinegar
- Sprinkle salt and pepper

Arrange some of the pre-sliced mozzarella slices on a platter. Add tomato slices on top of the mozzarella, sprinkle with salt, pepper and basil. Repeat layers. Drizzle with olive oil and balsamic vinegar. Refrigerate until ready to serve.

WARM SPINACH & PANCETTA SALAD

<u>Dressing:</u>

- ¼ pound pancetta, finely chopped (can also use bacon)
- ⅓ cup olive oil
- 3 tablespoons red wine vinegar
- ½ lemon, juiced
- ½ teaspoon black pepper

<u>Salad:</u>

- 1 bag (8 ounces) fresh baby spinach, cleaned
- 1/3 cup crumbled blue cheese (or more if you like)
- ¼ cup toasted pine nuts

Sauté pancetta in olive oil until crispy and golden, add vinegar, lemon juice and pepper. When ready to serve, toss in large bowl with spinach and sprinkle with cheese and pine nuts.

<u>Botto-Fischetti Tip:</u> *Sauté some thinly sliced mushrooms and onions with the pancetta is a nice addition.*

FRENCH DIP SANDWICH

- 2 tablespoons butter or olive oil
- 1 medium shallot, finely chopped
- 1 tablespoon flour
- 2 tablespoons dry white wine (optional)
- 2½ cups beef stock (or 2 cans beef broth)
- Dash of Worcestershire
- 1½ pounds cooked roast beef, thinly sliced (deli is fine)
- Sprinkle salt and pepper
- 4 sandwich rolls lightly toasted

Heat butter or oil over medium heat in a large shallow skillet; add shallots and sauté until translucent. Add flour and cook for a minute or two, whisk in wine followed by beef stock and Worcestershire. Bring to boil, reduce heat and allow simmering for 10 minutes.

When ready to serve, season meat with salt and pepper. Dip meat into sauce and pile on rolls, serve with remaining sauce in small bowls for dipping.

Botto-Fischetti Tip: *You can use dry sherry instead of wine.*

BBQ SLOPPY JOES

- 1-tablespoon olive or vegetable oil
- 1-pound ground beef
- ½ onion, chopped
- 1 large garlic clove, minced
- 1 teaspoon dry mustard (use regular yellow if that's all you have)
- ½ cup ketchup
- ¼ cup BBQ sauce
- ½ teaspoon chili powder (optional if you like a little heat)
- Salt and pepper to taste
- 4 toasted hamburger buns

Heat oil in large skillet, add meat, onion and garlic and cook breaking up with wooden spoon until meat is browned and cooked through, drain excess fat.

Add mustard, ketchup, BBQ sauce, chili powder, salt and pepper. Stir to combine well, cover and simmer for 20-30 minutes. Taste for seasoning, if needed, and serve on toasted buns.

Botto-Fischetti Tip: *You can always use turkey meat for a healthier option.*

Avocado & Chicken Cobb Salad

- 2 heads romaine lettuce, washed, dried and chopped
- 3 hard boiled eggs, peeled and chopped
- 2 boneless/skinless chicken breast halves, cooked and diced
- 3 tomatoes, diced
- 6 slices bacon, cooked crispy and chopped
- 1 avocado, peeled, pitted and diced
- ¾ cup Roquefort or blue cheese crumbles
- ¾ cup salad dressing (traditional is red wine vinaigrette)
- Sprinkle salt and pepper

Spread chopped lettuce on a large serving platter; arrange the eggs, chicken, tomato, bacon, avocado and cheese crumbles in rows on top of the lettuce. Season with salt and pepper.

Drizzle salad dressing over top and serve; alternatively, you can toss all ingredients in large bowl.

Botto-Fischetti Tip: *You can also use a rotisserie chicken to save time. Any dressing you like will work for this salad.*

GRILLED BEEF BURGERS

- 1½ pounds ground chuck (80/20 mix)
- 1 teaspoon Montreal steak seasoning or salt & pepper to taste
- Cheese if desired

Sprinkle meat with seasoning and mix together with your hands until just combined. Try not to overwork the meat as it becomes tough. Take 4-6 ounce portions depending on preferred serving size and shape into a patty, approximately 1 inch thick.

Preheat grill to medium high heat and place burgers on grill, close lid and cook for approximately 7-8 minutes on the first side. Burger is ready to flip when it releases from the grill easily. Do not press down on burger with spatula or juices will be released. Cook for another 4-5 minutes for medium or a little longer if you prefer more well done.

Lay cheese slice on for last minute of cooking to melt. Serve in bun of your liking with toppings.

Suggestions: bacon, mushrooms, lettuce, tomato, onion, pickle, BBQ sauce, mayo, mustard, ketchup, caramelized onions, relish, chili, jalapenos, guacamole.

CHEDDAR & MOZZARELLA GRILLED CHEESE

- 4-6 slices of ½ inch sourdough bread
- 4 tablespoons room temperature butter
- 5-ounces shredded mozzarella cheese
- 5-ounces shredded cheddar cheese
- Panini press or grill pan
- Cooking spray

Preheat the Panini maker. Spray cooking spray on your Panini maker or grill pan. Lay the sliced bread out and spread butter on both sides of the bread. Add the cheese mixture over bread.

Grill the sandwiches two at a time for 3-4 minutes until golden brown. Then cut them diagonally and enjoy eating your grilled cheese!

Botto-Fischetti Tip: *You can add any cheese, spinach, bacon, turkey or tomatoes in your grilled cheese sandwich. If you don't have a Panini press, you can make this with your skillet on your stove.*

ORGANIC CHICKEN & GRAPE SALAD SANDWICH

- 2 cups cooked organic chicken (shredded)
- ½ cup diced celery
- ½ cup halved red grapes
- ⅓ cup diced red onion
- ⅓ cup shredded carrots
- ½ cup mayonnaise
- 1½ tablespoons Dijon mustard
- 1 teaspoon celery salt
- ½ teaspoon black pepper
- 1 teaspoon garlic powder
- 1 teaspoon paprika
- 4-6 sandwich rolls

Combine all ingredients in a bowl and toss well. Keep refrigerated until ready to serve. Toast your sandwich roll and add lettuce, tomato and avocado for toppings.

Botto-Fischetti Tip: *To save you time use a rotisserie chicken that is already cooked.*

Coconut Vegetable Soup

- 1 15-ounce can cannellini beans, drained and rinsed
- 1 onion, chopped
- 2 carrots, peeled and chopped
- 2 zucchinis, chopped
- 1 garlic clove, chopped
- 1¼ teaspoons salt
- ½ teaspoon black pepper
- ½ tablespoon cumin
- 2 teaspoons sage, fresh or powder
- 1 tablespoon of Herbs de Provence
- 1 32-ounce box chicken broth
- 1 13.5-ounce can coconut milk
- 1 28-ounce can whole peeled tomatoes
- 2-3 cups of baby spinach (fresh)
- 2 tablespoons olive oil

In a bowl, mash half of the cannellini beans with a fork and set aside. Heat olive oil in a large pot over medium to high heat. Add onions, zucchini, carrots, garlic, sage, cumin, Herbs de Provence, salt and pepper. Mix well.

Cook vegetables until tender about 5-7 minutes. Add chicken broth, mashed cannellini beans, whole beans and tomatoes, bring to a boil. Reduce heat and simmer for 30 minutes. Add coconut milk, and spinach leaves the last 5 minutes of cooking. Taste for seasoning. Serve with crackers.

Botto-Fischetti Tip: _Great with quinoa or rice for a heartier meal._

WHITE BEAN SOUP WITH TINY MEATBALLS

For the soup:
- 1 tablespoon olive oil
- ½ tsp. crushed red pepper
- 1 medium yellow onion, finely chopped
- 1 carrot, diced
- 3 garlic cloves, minced
- 6 cups chicken broth
- 1 cup crushed tomatoes (canned are fine)
- ½ cup dry white wine
- 1 bay leaf
- 4 ounces fresh spinach, roughly cut (about ½ bag or couple handfuls)
- Salt and pepper to taste

For the meatballs:
- ½ pound ground beef
- 1 egg white
- 2 tablespoons chopped flat leaf parsley
- 2 tablespoons dry breadcrumbs
- 2 tablespoons grated parmesan cheese (plus more for serving)
- 1 can cannellini beans, drained and rinsed (about 2 cups)
- Salt and pepper to taste

In a large pot, heat the oil over medium low heat. Add the red pepper flakes, onion, carrot, and garlic. Cover and cook until tender, about 10 minutes. Add the stock, tomatoes, wine, and bay leaf and bring to a boil. Reduce the heat, cover, and simmer for 25 minutes.

Meanwhile make the meatballs. In a medium bowl, mix the beef, parsley, bread crumbs, Parmesan, ½ teaspoon salt, and ⅛ teaspoon black pepper. Shape into twenty-five tiny meatballs.

Add the beans and meatballs to the soup. Cover and simmer until meatballs are just done, about 5 to 7 minutes. Add the spinach, stir until just wilted, remove bay leaf and season to taste with salt and pepper. Serve sprinkled with Parmesan cheese.

Botto-Fischetti Tip: *Add al dente pre-cooked small shaped pasta with beans and meatballs to make heartier.*

GINGER CARROT SOUP

- 4-6 carrots, peeled and chopped in large pieces
- 1 large yellow onion, chopped (big chop)
- 2 tablespoons olive oil
- 1 tablespoon minced garlic
- 1½ tablespoons fresh grated ginger
- 1 teaspoon honey
- 1 tablespoon salt
- ¼ teaspoon black pepper
- 32-ounces vegetable broth
- Sprinkle red pepper flakes for spice (optional)
- ½ lime juice, squeezed fresh
- Dollop of crème fraiche for topping

In a large pot, heat olive oil on medium to high heat. Add onion, carrots, garlic and ginger sauté for 5 minutes. Add salt, black pepper, red pepper and sauté for another 10 minutes. Then add vegetable broth, honey, and lime juice and bring to a boil. Reduce heat and simmer on low until the carrots are fork tender, about 20-30 minutes.

Taste for seasoning. Use an immersion blender to blend the soup in the pot. Just make sure the soup is not too hot before you blend. Use a dollop of crème fraiche on top of your soup for topping.

Botto-Fischetti Tip: *You can use sour cream or tofu sour cream for your topping. A food processor works well in case you don't have a hand-held immersion blender.*

LUNCH SIDES

CHEESE PITA PIZZA

- 1-2 whole-wheat pita bread
- ½ cup jar marinara sauce (any kind you like)
- 2 tablespoons grated mozzarella cheese
- 2 tablespoons grated cheddar cheese
- 1 tomato, sliced thinly
- Sprinkle salt
- Sprinkle black pepper
- Cooking spray

Preheat oven to 400°F degrees. Spray baking sheet with cooking spray and place pita bread on. Spread the marinara sauce all over the pita bread. Sprinkle cheeses, salt, black pepper and sliced tomato over marinara sauce. Bake for 8-10 minutes until cheese is melted.

Botto-Fischetti Tip: *You can add any vegetables or cheese you like. You can also substitute marinara sauce for pesto sauce.*

GUACAMOLE

- 3 ripe avocados
- ½ cup diced red onion
- 2 limes, juiced
- ½ teaspoon cayenne pepper
- ½ teaspoon cumin powder
- 1 teaspoon salt
- 2 garlic cloves, minced
- ½ cup cherry tomatoes, diced
- 3 tablespoons olive oil

Cut avocados in half and remove pits. Scoop the avocado flesh into a bowl and mash with a fork leaving chunky. Squeeze lime juice over; add onions, salt, cayenne pepper, cumin, tomatoes, and olive oil. Toss well and taste for seasoning. Refrigerate before serving. Serve with chips!

Botto-Fischetti Tip: *You can add dashes of hot sauce, cilantro or lemon juice instead of limes.*

Salsa

- 3-4 large ripe tomatoes, diced
- ¼ red onion, diced
- 1 garlic clove, minced
- ⅓ - ½ of jalapeno, diced
- 3 tablespoons fresh lime juice
- 2 tablespoons chopped cilantro
- ½ teaspoon salt
- 1 tablespoon olive oil

Put all ingredients in a food processor and blend well. Keep in a refrigerator until ready to serve.

CHEESE QUESADILLA

- 4 cups (16 ounce) of grated cheese (Monterey jack, sharp or mild cheddar)
- 6" - 8" flour tortillas
- 1½ tablespoons butter

Melt ½ tablespoon of butter in a medium skillet, place a tortilla on the skillet and sprinkle evenly with 1 ⅓ cups of grated cheese (and any other filling you'd like to add). Cover pan and cook until tortilla is golden brown, and cheese is partially melted, flip and cook until golden brown on the other side. Repeat process. Cut into triangles and serve with salsa, sour cream and guacamole.

Botto-Fischetti Tip: *You can add many ingredients with the cheese to this basic recipe. Some additional suggestions: cooked diced chicken, beef or any other meat, diced green chilies, olives, grilled peppers, onions, mushrooms, additional hot sauce and/or seasonings, refried or black beans, corn, green onion, diced tomato, cilantro, bacon, spinach.*

HONEY VINAIGRETTE SALAD DRESSING

- 1 medium shallot, peeled and roughly chopped
- 1 teaspoon Dijon mustard
- 1 tablespoon red wine vinegar
- 2 tablespoons white wine vinegar
- 2 tablespoons honey
- 5 tablespoons olive oil
- ½ teaspoon salt
- ¼ teaspoon black pepper

Pour first 5 ingredients in blender, and then slowly drizzle in olive oil until combined. Salt and Pepper to taste.

Botto-Fischetti Tip: *Toss with mixed greens, spinach or any lettuce. Serve topped with chopped apple or pear, crumbled cheese (goat, feta, blue, etc.) and any dried fruits and nuts (toasted or spiced).*

ORZO PASTA DRESSING

- 1-2 garlic cloves, chopped or grated
- 1 tablespoon Dijon mustard
- 1 tablespoon honey
- 2 teaspoons balsamic vinegar
- 1 teaspoon sugar
- 1 cup olive oil
- Sprinkle salt and black pepper
- 1 pound orzo pasta (cook according to package)

Whisk all dressing ingredients together. Taste for seasoning. Refrigerate until ready to serve over cooked orzo pasta.

Botto-Fischetti Tip: *You can add this dressing with grilled asparagus and cherry tomatoes! You can eat this cold or warm.*

HOT ARTICHOKE DIP

- 1 14-ounce jar or a can of artichoke hearts, chopped (drain the liquid)
- 8-ounce package softened cream cheese
- 1 10.5-ounce can of cream of mushroom soup
- 1 jalapeno, diced
- 1½ cups cheddar cheese
- 1½ cups parmesan cheese (reserve 2 tablespoon for topping)
- Casserole dish

Preheat oven to 350°F degrees. Combine in a large bowl: artichokes, cream of mushroom, cream cheese, jalapeno, cheddar cheese, and Parmesan cheese. Mix together well. Pour into a baking dish and bake for 30-45 minutes or until bubbly. Serve with crackers or chips.

Botto-Fischetti Tip: *You can add caramelized onions and hot sauce to add additional flavor. If you are making for a crowd, double the recipe. Eat with crackers, chips or baguette slices.*

BASIC BALSAMIC VINAIGRETTE

- 1 teaspoon Dijon mustard
- ¼ cup balsamic vinegar
- 1½ teaspoon brown sugar (dark or light)
- 1 large garlic clove, minced
- ½ teaspoon salt
- ¼ teaspoon pepper
- ¾ cup olive oil

Combine mustard, vinegar, sugar, garlic, salt and pepper and mix well. Slowly add olive oil, whisking until thoroughly combined.

Botto-/Fischetti Tip: *Great dressing for any kind of salad.*

TOFU SOUR CREAM

- 1 10-ounce package of silken firm tofu (drained)
- 5 tablespoons olive oil
- 2 tablespoons fresh squeezed lemon juice
- 2 scallions, chopped
- 1 teaspoon sea salt
- 1 garlic clove, chopped
- 2 teaspoons apple cider vinegar
- Food processor

In a food processor, add all ingredients and blend until smooth and creamy. Taste for seasoning. Chill until ready to serve.

Botto-Fischetti Tip: *Great to serve with baked potato, chili, soups, pizza and dips.*

Dinner

Homemade Chicken Noodle Soup

- 3-4 chicken breast halves
- 3 carrots, peeled and diced
- 2 stalks celery, diced
- ¼ cup chopped parsley
- 1 12-ounce package of egg wide noodles
- 2-3 quarts chicken stock
- ½ teaspoon salt
- ¼ teaspoon black pepper
- 1-2 tablespoon olive oil

Preheat oven to 375°F degrees. Place chicken on a baking sheet and rub chicken with olive oil and salt and pepper. Roast for 45 minutes until cooked through (no pink inside).

Once the chicken has cooled down, shred all the chicken meat and put aside. Bring chicken stock to a boil, reduce to simmer. Add celery and carrots. Once, the carrots and celery are tender, add the noodles.

Simmer uncovered until the noodles are tender, add your shredded chicken and parsley and heat through. Season to taste!

Botto-Fischetti Tip: *Squeeze lemon for taste! Buy rotisserie chicken to save you some time.*

TERIYAKI CHICKEN LEGS

- 8 chicken pieces (legs & thighs work best)
- ½ to ⅔ cup flour
- ½ cup teriyaki sauce (Yoshida's a good brand)

Preheat oven to 425°F degrees. Put flour in a plastic bag, add chicken pieces a couple at a time and shake until coated. Lay in a single layer on a baking sheet so the pieces are not touching each other. Bake in the oven for about 1 hour until crispy and cooked through. Toss with sauce and serve.

Botto-Fischetti Tip: *For easier cleanup, cover baking sheet with aluminum foil.*

PESTO CHICKEN KABOBS

- 4 boneless skinless chicken breast halves, cubed into 1" pieces
- ½ cup prepared pesto sauce, plus additional for serving
- 1 red bell pepper, cut into approx. ½" squares
- 2 pints cherry tomatoes
- Salt & pepper to taste
- Metal or wire kabob skewers

Place chicken breast pieces in a resalable plastic bag, then add ½ cup pesto sauce. Seal bag and swoosh around until chicken is well coated. Marinate in refrigerator 1/2 hour to 2 hours.

Thread chicken on skewers, alternating with pepper pieces and cherry tomato. Salt & pepper to taste. Grill over medium heat until chicken is cooked through, approx. 5-7 minutes per side. Drizzle with extra sauce and serve.

Botto-Fischetti Tip: *Use different colored peppers and tomatoes for a prettier dish!*

HONEY MUSTARD SALMON

- 1½ - 2 pounds salmon fillet
- 1 tablespoon Dijon mustard
- 1 tablespoon whole grain mustard
- 1 tablespoon honey
- 1 tablespoon finely chopped dill
- 3 tablespoons olive oil
- 2 garlic cloves, chopped
- Zest of one lemon
- Salt and pepper to taste
- Baking sheet
- Cooking spray

Preheat oven to 400°F degrees. In a small dish combine the mustards, honey, dill, olive oil, garlic and lemon zest, mix well. Lightly salt and pepper salmon.

Transfer salmon onto foil covered baking sheet and pour mustard mixture over salmon. Bake for 10-15 minutes or until its white and flaky.

Botto-Fischetti Tip: *It tastes best if you marinade it overnight in the refrigerator. Any left over, use in your salad for next day lunch.*

TOMATO, BASIL, AND SPINACH PASTA

- 3 tablespoons olive oil
- 1 medium onion, diced
- 3 large cloves garlic, minced
- ½ teaspoon crushed red pepper
- 3-4 chopped Roma tomatoes
- 4-5 ounces fresh spinach, cut into ribbons
- ½ cup chopped basil
- ½ cup toasted pine nuts
- 1 teaspoon salt
- 1 pound linguine pasta, cooked according to package directions

Heat olive oil in a large sauté pan on medium heat; add onion and garlic and sauté until onion is translucent. Add salt, crushed red pepper and tomatoes, cook 3-4 minutes or until tomatoes start to break down.

Add spinach, basil and pine nuts and mix well. Season to taste. Toss with freshly cooked pasta and serve with cheese.

Botto-Fischetti Tip: *You can use Kale salad, and any kind of pasta you like. Save a little (⅓-½ cup) of the pasta cooking water and add when combining pasta and/or veggies.*

Soy Sauce & Honey Tri-Tip Roast

- 3-4 pounds tri-tip roast, excess fat trimmed
- 2-3 tablespoons olive oil
- 2-3 garlic cloves, chopped
- ¼ cup honey
- ½ cup soy sauce
- ½ teaspoon red pepper flakes (if you like it spicy)
- 1 teaspoon salt
- ½ teaspoon black pepper
- 1 teaspoon ginger powder
- Zest of 1 lemon
- Ziploc bag
- Grill pan
- Cooking spray

Pour all ingredients in a Ziploc bag and marinate from 2 hours to overnight. Bring your steak to room temperature before grilling.

Spray the grill pan with cooking spray and have the grill on medium to high heat. Put your roast onto the hot grill, and cook approx. 12-15 minutes per side. Depending how you like your meat, will determine to cook longer or less (approx. 20-35 minutes total cooking time).

Let your steaks rest for at least 20 minutes before slicing across the grain.

Botto-Fischetti Tip: *You can make steak sandwiches with leftovers!*

GRILLED TEQUILA & LIME FISH TACOS

- 1 pound mild white fish such as tilapia, Mahi-Mahi or Cod

Marinade:

- 1 lime, zest and juiced
- 2 tablespoons vegetable oil
- 2 tablespoons tequila
- 1 jalapeno, seeded and coarsely chopped
- 1 teaspoon cumin
- 1 teaspoon chili powder
- ¼ cup chopped fresh cilantro leaves
- ½ teaspoon salt
- ¼ teaspoon pepper

Place fish in a medium size shallow dish. Combine all marinade ingredients and pour over fish, let marinate for 15-20 minutes. Remove fish from marinade and grill over hot grill approximately 3-4 minutes per side until flaky.

Serve on corn or flour tortillas with desired toppings: Cabbage slaw, lettuce, salsa, sour cream, guacamole, cheese, and additional chopped cilantro.

BAKED MAC & CHEESE

- 6 tablespoons butter
- 4½ cups warm whole milk
- ½ cup flour
- 1 teaspoon dry mustard
- ½ teaspoon cayenne pepper
- ½ teaspoon salt
- ½ teaspoon black pepper
- ¼ teaspoon Worchester sauce
- Dash hot sauce (optional)
- 4 cups (16oz) grated sharp cheddar cheese
- 1 pound macaroni pasta, cooked as directed on package
- 1½ cups crushed potato chips or breadcrumbs
- ½ cup of parmesan cheese for topping

Heat oven to 350°F degrees. Melt butter in a large saucepan over medium heat. Whisk in flour and cook for about 1 minute. Whisk in the warm milk and bring to a boil, stirring constantly. The mixture will thicken as you stir.

Add dry mustard, cayenne, salt, pepper, hot sauce and Worchester. Stir in 4 cups of cheddar cheese until it melts. Pour the cheese sauce over the pasta in a large casserole dish. Sprinkle the potato chips and Parmesan cheese over the top and bake uncovered for 35-45 minutes until golden brown and bubbly.

BAKED PARMESAN GARLIC BREAD

- 1 loaf French bread split in half

Topping:

- 1 cup mayonnaise
- ¾ cup grated Asiago cheese
- ½ cup grated parmesan cheese
- 3-4 tablespoons minced garlic cloves
- ¼ teaspoon black pepper
- Handful of parsley chopped
- Sprinkle of paprika

Preheat oven to 400°F degrees. Mix all topping ingredients together (except paprika) and spread over the sliced loaf of bread. Sprinkle paprika on top. Place garlic bread on a baking sheet and place in the oven for 5-10 minutes until the top is golden brown.

Keep checking your oven, so you won't burn your garlic bread.

DUTCH OVEN CHICKEN BAKE

- 4-6 pieces chicken
- 2 tablespoons olive oil
- 1 onion, sliced
- 1-2 carrots, sliced diagonally
- 3 whole garlic cloves
- 1 can cream of mushroom condensed soup
- 1 can of cream of celery condensed soup
- 1½ cups white rice
- 3½ cups chicken broth
- ½ tablespoon salt
- ½ tablespoon thyme
- ½ teaspoon black pepper
- Handful of chopped fresh parsley

Preheat oven to 350°F degrees. In a Dutch oven pot heat olive oil over medium high heat. Sprinkle salt and pepper on the chicken. Add the chicken pieces to the pot and sauté the chicken on both sides until golden brown. Add onions, carrots, garlic, and thyme.

In a bowl, mix together with rice and the cans of mushrooms and celery soup. Pour over the chicken and add chicken broth over the chicken mixture. Remove from heat, cover the Dutch oven pot with lid and bake for 2 hours. Serve with fresh parsley for garnish.

Botto-Fischetti Tip: *You can make this in a crock-pot as well.*

CAPER & TUNA RIGATONI PASTA

- ¼ cup olive oil
- 2 large cloves of garlic, minced
- ¼ - ½ teaspoon red pepper flakes crushed, depending on heat preference
- 2 cans tuna, drained (oil or water packed)
- 1 cup chicken stock
- 3 tablespoons capers, drained
- Sprinkle salt and pepper to taste
- 1 pound pasta – ziti, penne or similar (cooked to package directions)
- 1 cup of grated parmesan cheese

Heat olive oil in a medium size pot, over medium low heat. Add garlic and red pepper flakes and sauté for 30 seconds until fragrant. Add tuna, chicken stock and capers. Stir to breakup tuna and heat through. Toss with hot pasta, adjust seasonings and serve with cheese.

Botto-Fischetti Tip: *For best flavor toss pasta and sauce together over medium high heat for 30 seconds to 1 minute.*

Tuna Mushroom Casserole

- 1 tablespoon vegetable oil
- ⅓ cup minced onion
- 1 can cream of mushroom soup
- 1-1½ cups of milk
- ½ teaspoon Worcestershire sauce
- 2½ cups crushed regular potato chips (approx. ½ of 10.5oz bag)
- 2 cans tuna, (drained)
- 1½ cups frozen peas
- 1½ cups rice

Preheat oven to 350°F. Layer 1 cup of crushed chips in bottom of 13x9 baking dish; crumble drained tuna over the top. Sauté onion in oil in a pot over medium heat, add soup, milk and Worcestershire sauce and heat through stirring until thoroughly combined. Pour over top of tuna and sprinkle remaining 1 ½ cups of chips over.

Bake at 350°F for 20 minutes or until bubbly and golden brown on top. Meanwhile, cook rice and peas according to package directions and serve together.

LEMON GINGER TILAPIA

- 2-4 tilapia fish fillets (4 to 6 ounces each fish)
- 1 cup coconut milk
- 1 lemon, zested and juiced
- ¾ cup chopped parsley
- 1 teaspoon salt
- ½ teaspoon black pepper
- 1 teaspoon fresh ginger or ginger powder
- 2 garlic cloves, chopped
- ½ teaspoon minced jalapeno pepper (optional)
- Squeeze lime

Preheat oven to 425°F degrees. Combine coconut milk, lemon, salt, black pepper, ginger, garlic and jalapeno in a blender and pulse until smooth.

Pour mixture over the fish in a casserole dish and bake covered for 10 minutes. Uncover and bake for an additional 5 minutes until the fish is opaque in the center. Squeeze lime over for finishing touch.

Botto-/Fischetti Tip: *Serve with rice and veggies!*

BRUSSELS SPROUTS & BUTTERNUT SQUASH

- 1½ pounds Brussel sprouts, washed and cut in half
- 1 pound butternut squash cubes (1 small squash)
- 2-4 tablespoons olive oil
- ½ cup toasted pecans, chopped
- 1 cup dried cranberries
- 3 tablespoons brown sugar
- 1 teaspoon of salt
- 1 teaspoon of black pepper
- Cooking spray
- Balsamic glaze to finish

Preheat oven to 400°F degrees. In a bowl combine Brussel sprouts, butternut squash cubes, olive oil, brown sugar, salt and pepper. Toss well. Spray baking sheet with cooking spray. Transfer Brussel-sprouts, and butternut squash mixture onto the baking sheet.

Bake for 45- 60 minutes until golden brown. Once the Brussel-sprouts and squash are finished cooking, add the toasted pecans and cranberries and mix well. Drizzle the balsamic glaze over the Brussel sprouts and butternut squash mixture as a topping and serve.

Botto-Fischetti Tip: *You can add toasted pine nuts, pomegranate, bacon or pancetta to this dish. Buy your Brussel sprouts and butternut squash already pre-cut for you.*

ORZO PASTA PILAF

- 2½ tablespoons butter
- ½ cup minced yellow onion
- 1 cup orzo pasta
- 2 cups chicken or vegetable stock
- 2 handfuls fresh spinach leaves, chopped
- ¼ cup slivered almonds, toasted
- Salt and pepper to taste

In large pot, melt butter over medium high heat. Add onion, pasta and sauté until pasta is lightly toasted (about 3-5 minutes). Add stock, salt, and pepper to taste and bring to a boil.

Reduce heat to low, cover and cook until pasta is tender and the liquid is absorbed. Cook about 12-15 minutes. Remove cover, add spinach the last 5 minutes and stir until wilted. Finish off with toasted nuts. Taste for seasoning.

Botto-Fischetti Tip: *Sliced mushrooms sautéed with onions is a nice addition! You can also add scallions for the finishing touch.*

VEGETABLE & RICE BOWL

- 1 small eggplant, chopped
- 2 cups diced cauliflower
- Yellow onion, chopped
- 1 bell pepper, chopped (any color)
- Garlic cloves, finely diced
- 1½ cup of rice (any kind you like)
- 3-4 tablespoons olive oil
- 3 cups of vegetable broth
- 1 teaspoon of salt
- ½ teaspoon of black pepper
- 1 teaspoon Italian seasoning
- ½ teaspoon ginger powder

Heat olive oil in a large pot over medium high heat; add onion, garlic eggplant, cauliflower and bell pepper. Add spices and mix well. Sauté vegetables until fork tender. Add rice and vegetable broth to the vegetable mixture.

Bring to a boil, then simmer on low until all the liquid is absorbed about 20-25 minutes for white rice (45-55 minutes if using brown rice). Taste for seasoning.

Botto-Fischetti Tip: *You can use any vegetables you have on hand. If you don't have rice, use quinoa, or pasta noodles and adjust cooking time as needed.*

BALSAMIC SALMON GLAZE

- 4 salmon fillets
- 1 teaspoon salt
- 1 teaspoon black pepper
- 1 teaspoon fresh or ginger spice
- 2 -3 teaspoons vegetable oil

Glaze:

- ¼ cup balsamic vinegar
- ¼ cup water
- 1½ tablespoon lemon juice (fresh is best)
- 2 tablespoons brown sugar

Stir together vinegar, brown sugar, and lemon juice in a small bowl. Pat salmon dry, and add salt, pepper, and ginger.

Heat the oil in a nonstick skillet over medium high heat and add salmon and sear for about 4-5 minutes on each side until salmon is cooked through.

Take the vinegar mixture, let it bubble and then let it simmer until it thickens and is reduced by ⅓ cup. Spoon glaze over salmon.

CHICKEN STIR FRY

- 4 boneless skinless chicken breast halves, cut into ½" cubes
- 3 tablespoons peanut oil
- 1 cup bottled teriyaki sauce
- ¼ cup soy sauce
- 2 garlic cloves, minced
- 4 green onions, chopped (plus extra for garnish)
- 1 cup frozen peas (don't thaw)
- 1 cup frozen cubed carrots (don't thaw)
- 5 eggs lightly beaten
- 6 cups cooked white rice or brown rice

Add garlic to the teriyaki sauce and marinate the chicken in the mixture for 20 -30 minutes.

Heat a large skillet with 2 tablespoons of oil on high heat. Add chicken, reserving marinade and cook chicken until no longer pink inside. Remove and set aside.

Heat additional tablespoon of oil in skillet, add rice, green onion, peas and carrots and stir fry for 3-4 minutes until heated through. Add eggs and stir until scrambled and cooked through. Add ½ cup of the reserved teriyaki mixture (discard rest), soy sauce and reserved chicken, mix together well and serve garnished with additional green onion.

Botto-Fischetti Tip: *This is a great dish to make vegetarian by replacing chicken with tofu.*

Tofu Veggie Pizza

- 1 pizza thin crust (store bought)
- 4 tablespoons olive oil
- 1 cup chopped firm tofu
- 1 cup sliced mushrooms
- 1 cup broccoli florets
- 1 cup chopped kale
- 1 cup grated mozzarella cheese
- Sprinkle salt
- Sprinkle crushed red pepper flakes (optional)
- 2 basil leaves, chopped
- Balsamic glaze for topping
- Cooking spray

Preheat oven to 400°F degrees. Use cooking spray on your baking sheet. Roll your pizza crust on the baking sheet. Brush 2 tablespoon of olive oil over the pizza crust. Spread all your vegetables, tofu, and cheese over your pizza crust. Add salt, red pepper flakes, and basil. Drizzle the remaining 2 tablespoons of olive oil over the pizza.

Bake for 15-20 minutes. Once, the pizza is done, drizzle balsamic glaze over and serve.

Botto-Fischetti Tip: *You can add any vegetable or cheese you like. Great to top tofu sour cream over it.*

RIB-EYE STEAK

- 2 each 1¼ inch rib-eye steaks
- 2 tablespoon vegetable oil
- 1 tablespoon salt
- ½ tablespoon black pepper

Bring steaks to room temperature and rub with salt and pepper. Heat cast iron skillet to medium-high heat. Add the vegetable oil. Then add the steaks to the skillet; they should begin to sizzle immediately. If not, your pan is not hot enough, remove and heat further.

Cook steaks on each side for 3-5 minutes for medium rare. Cook longer if you like it medium or well done.

DINNER SIDES

PIZZA SAUCE

- 3 tablespoons olive oil
- 1 medium onion, chopped
- 3 garlic cloves, minced
- 1 28-ounce can crushed tomatoes
- 1 6-ounce can tomato paste
- 2 teaspoons dried oregano (or 2 tablespoons fresh)
- ½ teaspoon of sugar
- Pinch of red pepper flakes (optional)
- 8-10 fresh basil leaves, chopped
- Salt & pepper to taste

Heat olive oil in a medium sauté pan over medium heat, add onion, and cook until translucent. Add garlic and cook until fragrant, about 1 minute. Add crushed tomatoes, tomato paste, oregano, sugar, red pepper if using and season with salt & pepper. Stir well and bring to a boil, reduce heat and cook until thick, approximately 30 min.

Add basil and adjust seasonings to taste. Makes about 5 cups.

Botto-Fischetti Tip: *You can also use this sauce for any pasta you like. You can buy store bought pizza dough.*

Ginger Chicken Marinade

- 4-6 pieces chicken thighs (you can use any kind of chicken)
- 2 garlic cloves, chopped
- 1 teaspoon fresh grated ginger
- 1 teaspoon salt
- 1 teaspoon black pepper
- 1 cup teriyaki sauce
- 1 large Ziploc bag

Mix all of these ingredients in a bowl and pour over chicken. Put in Ziploc bag and refrigerate for 30 minutes to overnight.

Botto-Fischetti Tip: *Great to grill, cook in the oven or stovetop.*

LEMON ZEST BROCCOLI

- 1½ pounds broccoli florets, cut into half size pieces
- 1½ teaspoons salt
- ½ teaspoon black pepper
- ½ teaspoon red pepper flakes
- Juice and zest of ½ lemon
- 2-3 tablespoons of olive oil

Boil water in a large pot on medium high heat and add broccoli florets. Cook for 3-5 minutes until tender. Drain the broccoli. Have a bowl with ice water ready and immediately add the cooked broccoli to it to shock it for a couple of seconds. Drain the broccoli in it and put back into the pot. Add the rest of the ingredients and mix well. Taste for seasoning.

Botto-Fischetti Tip: *You can also add 2 tablespoons of soy sauce, and crushed garlic. You can also roast this in a 400°F degree oven and squeeze fresh lemon on it.*

ROASTED CAULIFLOWER

- 1 head cauliflower, cut into 1½-inch florets (or bag frozen cauliflower)
- 2-3 tablespoon olive oil
- 1-teaspoon salt
- ½ teaspoon black pepper
- Half to full lemon squeezed

Preheat oven to 400°F degrees. In a large bowl toss cauliflower, olive oil, salt and pepper. Spread a single layer on a baking sheet. Roast cauliflower in the oven for about 45-50 minutes or until lightly golden brown. Squeeze fresh lemon juice over once the cauliflower is removed from the oven and serve.

ROASTED RED POTATOES

- 1½ pounds red potatoes, (keep the skin on) washed and cut in quarters
- ½ teaspoon salt
- ¼ teaspoon black pepper
- 1 tablespoon garlic powder
- 1 tablespoon chopped fresh rosemary
- 1 tablespoon chopped fresh dill
- 3-4 tablespoons of olive oil
- Cooking spray

Preheat oven to 400°F degrees. In a large bowl, toss potatoes with remaining ingredients until well coated. Spray cooking spray on baking sheet and place potatoes in a single layer, skin side up. Bake for 45 minutes, turning once halfway through cooking until golden brown. Season to taste.

Botto-Fischetti Tip: *If you don't have fresh herbs, you can use dry ones.*

SAUTÉED SPINACH

- 1 8-ounce bag spinach
- 2 garlic cloves, minced
- ½ teaspoon dried nutmeg
- 2 tablespoons olive oil
- ½ teaspoon salt
- ¼ teaspoon black pepper

Sauté garlic in olive oil over medium heat for 30 seconds or until fragrant. Add spinach and nutmeg, salt and pepper and stir well until spinach is wilted. Taste for seasoning!

Botto-Fischetti Tip: *If you do not have olive oil you can use butter.*

BBQ BAKED STEAK FRIES

- 4 large russet potatoes cut into thick fries (keep skins on)
- 3-4 tablespoons olive oil
- 3 teaspoons BBQ seasoning mix (McCormick's Grill Mates or make your own blend)

Preheat oven to 400°F degrees. Spread potatoes onto a baking sheet, drizzle with olive oil and BBQ seasoning. Bake for 20 minutes, increase oven temp to 425°F and bake for another 20 minutes until brown and crispy. Taste for seasoning when it's done.

Botto-Fischetti Tip: *Don't overcrowd your steak fries on the baking sheet. Sprinkle some kosher salt when the fries are done.*

MASHED POTATOES

- 3 pounds potatoes, peeled and cubed (can use any variety)
- 1 cup heavy cream
- 1 stick (½ cup) butter
- Salt and pepper to taste

Boil potatoes in large pot of salted water until tender. Drain and mash with masher in a large bowl. Heat cream and butter together. Combine with mashed potatoes and season to taste.

Botto-Fischetti Tip: *Can use ½ and ½ milk, or any combination to reduce calories.*

GARLIC AND LEMON GREEN BEANS

- 1½ pounds green beans, ends trimmed
- 1 tablespoon olive oil
- 2 tablespoons butter
- 2 garlic cloves, minced
- ½ teaspoon red pepper flakes
- ½ tablespoon lemon zest (yellow peel only)
- Salt & Pepper to taste

Blanch green beans: Bring a large pot of salted water to a boil, add beans and cook until bright green (about 3-5 minutes). Drain and immediately add to a large bowl of ice water to stop cooking and cool. Drain beans well.

In sauté pan large enough to hold beans, heat oil and butter over medium heat until butter is melted. Add garlic and red pepper flakes, sauté until fragrant. Add beans and continue to sauté, stirring until beans are well coated with butter/garlic and heated through, about 5 minutes. Add lemon zest and season to taste with salt and pepper.

ITALIAN CHICKEN DRESSING

- 4 -6 pieces of chicken thighs or (any kind of chicken you like)
- ½ cup of bottled Italian salad dressing
- ½ teaspoon salt
- ½ teaspoon pepper
- 1 teaspoon paprika
- Ziploc bag

Preheat oven to 375°F. Put chicken in a Ziploc bag and pour Italian dressing, add spices. Marinate from 1 hour up to overnight. Place chicken with marinade in a casserole dish and bake in the oven for 45-55 minutes. Make sure chicken is cooked throughout, no pink inside.

Botto-Fischetti Tip: *You can always freeze this recipe and defrost the night before to be able to bake it.*

DIJON COCKTAIL SHRIMP SAUCE

- 1 package frozen deveined cooked shrimp
- ½ cup ketchup
- 3 tablespoons horseradish
- 1 tablespoon Dijon mustard
- 1 teaspoon Worchester sauce
- 1 teaspoon Tabasco sauce (add more drops if you like it spicy)
- ½ lemon, juiced

Mix all ingredients together and refrigerate until ready to serve. Defrost shrimp in colander and drain. Arrange shrimp on a platter and serve with cocktail sauce.

TWICE-BAKED BACON POTATOES

- 6 large russet potatoes, scrubbed clean
- 1 stick butter, melted
- 1 cup sour cream
- ¼ cup milk or cream
- 1 cup (4oz) grated cheese (cheddar, Jack or combination) plus more for topping
- 4 slices cooked bacon, crumbled
- 3 green onions, thinly sliced (white & light green parts only)
- Salt & Pepper to taste

Preheat oven to 400°F, poke potatoes several times with a fork to allow steam to escape. Place potatoes on the rack and bake until tender when pierced with a knife (approx. 1 hour depending on size). Remove from oven and reduce temperature to 375°F.

Cut potatoes in half and scoop out centers leaving a thin shell. Place shells skin side down on a baking sheet. Mash the potato centers in large mixing bowl; add melted butter, sour cream, milk and 1 cup grated cheese combining well. Add salt and pepper to taste. Mound filling into shells, top with bacon bits, sliced green onions and additional grated cheese.

Bake 15-20 minutes until heated through and cheese is melted, serve.

SPICY ITALIAN DIP

- 1-2 tablespoons minced garlic, depending on your taste
- 2 tablespoons chopped Italian parsley
- ¼ to 1 teaspoon red pepper flakes, depending on your taste
- 3 tablespoons balsamic vinegar
- ¼ cup olive oil
- Salt to taste

Mix all ingredients together and taste for seasoning. Serve with fresh baked bread for dipping.

SWEET TREATS & SNACKS

SNACKING ON HEALTHY NUTS

- 2 egg whites (no yolk)
- 1 teaspoon curry powder
- 1 teaspoon cayenne pepper
- 1 teaspoon salt
- ½ cup brown sugar
- ¼ cup honey
- ½ -1 cup almonds, walnuts, or pecans (any nuts you have) or use all three nuts
- Parchment paper

Preheat oven to 350°F degrees. Mix egg whites in a bowl. In a separate bowl, combine nuts, curry, cayenne pepper, salt, brown sugar, and honey. Add egg whites to the nut mixture and toss well. Place parchment paper on the baking sheet. Toss the nut mixture on top of the baking sheet and spread it out evenly.

Place in the oven and bake for 12-15 minutes or until it is lightly golden brown. Let it cool. Crumble it up and enjoy snacking.

Botto-Fischetti Tip: *You can add turmeric instead of curry. You can use any nuts you like.*

No Bake Protein Power Balls

- 2 tablespoons chia seeds
- 2 tablespoons flax seed
- 2 tablespoons sunflower seeds (optional)
- 2 tablespoons brown sugar or coconut sugar
- 3 tablespoons peanut butter
- 2 teaspoons cinnamon
- 1 teaspoon vanilla extract
- 1¼ cups of oats
- ½ cup grated carrots (buy packaged)
- ¼ cup walnuts or pecans chopped (or any nuts you have)
- ¼ cup honey
- ¼ cup of chocolate chips (optional)
- 2-3 tablespoon coconut oil

In a medium size bowl mix all ingredients together, except for coconut oil. Heat coconut oil in the microwave for 15 seconds until melted. Pour the melted coconut oil over all the ingredients. Mix all of the ingredients together until the mixture is well coated. Then refrigerate for 15-20 minutes.

Grab a small hand size and squeeze the mixture tightly and roll them up into tight balls. Keep refrigerated until ready to eat them.

Botto-Fischetti Tip: *Use any seeds you have. Great for before or after a workout.*

BAKED NUTMEG & CINNAMON STUFFED APPLES

- 4 apples (any kind you like)
- ¼ cup brown sugar
- 1 teaspoon cinnamon
- 1 teaspoon nutmeg
- ¼ cup honey
- ¼ cup golden raisins
- ¼ cup pecans or walnuts
- 1 cup apple cider vinegar
- 4 tablespoons of softened butter
- Casserole dish

Preheat oven to 375°F degrees. Wash and core apples, leaving the core at the bottom of the apples. In a bowl, mix brown sugar, cinnamon, nutmeg, honey, butter, raisins, and walnuts together and stuff into the apple cores. Fill the casserole with 1 cup of apple cider vinegar and place the apples in the casserole. Bake for an hour until the apples are soft and the apple mixture is bubbling.

Botto-Fischetti Tip: *You can slice the apples without going through the bottom of it, if you can't core the apple. Great with granola and vanilla ice cream as finished toppings.*

Cinnamon Sugar Mini Muffins

- 1 cup all-purpose flour
- 1½ teaspoons baking powder
- ½ teaspoon salt
- ½ stick (¼ cup) unsalted butter, softened
- ⅓ cup sugar
- 1 large egg
- ⅓ cup milk (whole, skim or buttermilk)
- 1 teaspoon vanilla

Topping:

- ¼ cup sugar
- 1 teaspoon cinnamon

Preheat oven to 375°F and line 24 mini muffin tins.

Make topping: In a small bowl or shaker stir together sugar and cinnamon.

Sift flour, baking powder and salt together into a bowl, set aside. Mix together milk and vanilla, set aside. In a bowl using an electric mixer, beat together butter and sugar until light and fluffy. Beat in egg until well combined.

Gently stir in flour mixture and add milk mixture, mixing until just combined. Divide batter evenly among cups and sprinkle with topping. Bake muffins in middle of oven 12 to 15 minutes or until tester comes out clean. Remove from pie tin and cool on rack. Makes 24 mini muffins.

Botto-Fischetti Tip: *Use a small ice cream scoop to evenly divide batter.*

CHOCOLATE CAKE

Sift together in large bowl:

- 2 cups all-purpose flour
- 2 cups sugar
- ¾ cup unsweetened cocoa powder
- ½ teaspoon salt
- 2 teaspoons baking soda
- 1 teaspoon baking powder

Add:

- 1 cup strong black coffee
- ½ cup vegetable oil
- 1 teaspoon vanilla extract
- ½ teaspoon almond extract
- 1 cup buttermilk
- 2 eggs

Heat oven to 350°F. Grease well and flour two 9-inch round baking pans or one 13x9x2-inch baking pan. Mix until smooth (batter will be thin). Pour into prepared pans, bake 30 to 35 minutes for round pans, 35 to 40 minutes for rectangular pan or until wooden pick inserted in center comes out clean. Cool 10 minutes. Loosen cake from side of pan and remove from pans to wire racks. Cool completely.

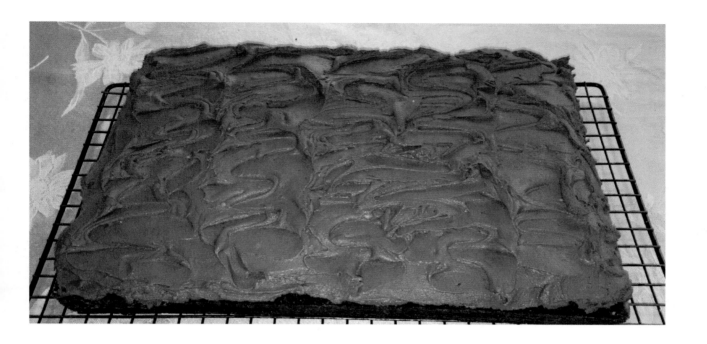

___**Botto-Fischetti Tip:**___ *Make sure to grease pans well - very moist and delicious!*

Banana Chocolate Chip Cookies

- ½ cup brown sugar
- ½ cup granulated sugar
- ¾ cup unsalted butter, at room temp
- 2 overripe bananas, mashed
- 1 teaspoon pure vanilla extract
- 1 large egg
- 1¾ cup rolled oats
- 1½ cup flour
- ½ teaspoon baking soda
- ½ teaspoon cinnamon
- ½ teaspoon salt
- 1½ cup milk chocolate chips

Preheat the oven to 350°F. In a large mixing bowl, mix together the sugar and butter until light and fluffy. Add the bananas and egg, combining well and then add the vanilla.

In a separate bowl mix oat, flour, baking soda, cinnamon, and salt until thoroughly combined. Add wet ingredients to dry ingredients and mix well. Stir in the chocolate chips. Scoop golf sized balls of dough onto ungreased baking sheet. Bake for 18-22 minutes until golden brown, cool on a wire rack.

Botto-Fischetti Tip: *Great with a glass of milk!*

BROWNIE NUGGETS

- 6 ounces semi-sweet chocolate morsels (about 1 cup)
- ½ cup mini chocolate chips
- 1 stick (½ cup) unsalted butter
- ½ cup plus 2 tablespoons flour
- ¼ teaspoon salt
- 2 large eggs
- ¾ cup packed light brown sugar
- 1 tsp. vanilla
- Sprinkle confectioners' sugar (optional)
- Muffin cup paper liners

Preheat oven to 350°F and line 24 mini-muffin cups with paper liners.

Slowly melt butter and chocolate chips together in the microwave (heat for only a few seconds at a time or on reduced power) stirring until smooth; set aside. Beat eggs and sugar with mixer until thick and pale. Add vanilla and melted chocolate to the mixture. Stir in salt and flour until just combined.

Spoon into muffin tin liners, filling them just to the top. Bake for 15 minutes or until edges are set but centers are still moist and fudgy. Sprinkle with confectioner's sugar before serving. Makes 24 brownie nuggets.

CHOCOLATE DIPPED STRAWBERRIES

- 8-ounce chocolate chips or chopped chocolate (dark or milk)
- 1-pound strawberries (about 20)

Wash the berries and dry completely, do not hull or remove the stems. In a microwave-safe bowl or measuring cup melt the chocolate chips on low for 1 minute, stir and then microwave for 15 second intervals, stirring in between until completely melted and smooth. Be very careful not to overheat.

Line a baking tray with waxed or parchment paper. Holding each strawberry by stem dip into the chocolate, lift out and let excess drip off. Set onto waxed paper and repeat with rest of berries. Set aside until chocolate hardens.

Botto-Fischetti Tip: *You can do this with other fruits (bananas, dried mango, cherries) nuts, pretzels, marshmallows, cookies, etc.*

HONEY, LIME, AND BASIL FRUIT SALAD

- 2 cups honeydew, cut in chunks
- 2 cups strawberries, sliced
- 1 cup of raspberries
- 1 cup of blueberries

Dressing:

- 2 tablespoons honey
- 3 tablespoons fresh lime juice
- 1 tablespoon lime zest
- 3 tablespoons fresh basil leaves, chopped

Place all fruit in a bowl. Whisk dressing ingredients together and toss with fruit. Place in the refrigerator until ready to serve.

Botto-Fischetti Tip: *You can always add yogurt as a topping. Or make a smoothie with leftovers.*

STRAWBERRY BANANA CRÈME FRAICHE

- ½ cup crème fraiche
- 1-tablespoon coconut sugar
- ½ tablespoon honey
- 1 banana sliced
- ¼ cup strawberries sliced
- ½ teaspoon lemon zest (plus additional for garnish)

In a bowl mix crème fraiche, sugar, honey and lemon zest all together. Put your sliced fruit in a dessert bowl and pour the crème fraiche mixture over your fruit. Top with more lemon zest.

Botto-Fischetti Tip: *You can add chocolate syrup and granola over the top as well. This can work with any fruit.*

ACKNOWLEDGEMENT PAGE

I cannot express enough how thankful I am to my family for all of the support, guidance, and patience they have given me in finalizing this project. The inspiring days of cooking and testing the recipes were exciting, creative, and exhausting at times. There were days where you could not cook one more thing, but at the end of it, I would not change a thing!

I would like to thank my co-author Tammy Fischetti for all of her hard work and her loyal dedication to get this book ready to launch. We have been cooking together for many years, and trying-out many different recipes dealing with picky eaters. Having our children grow up and experience college together made us realize our children needed and missed "their moms cooking". It was this thought from our children that started our college cookbook experience. Thank you, Tammy and your three sons Ricky, Paul, and Anthony for all your support and patience with getting Chomp College Cookbook up and going.

I would like to thank my wonderful parents, especially my mom, for teaching me how to cook and showing me the love of the kitchen. I also want to thank my mother-in-law who showed me how to prepare foods in advance, and my talented sister-in-law, the baker, for always supporting me and showing me the tricks of the trade when it comes to all kinds of goodies in the kitchen.

A very special gratitude goes to my three sisters, my brother, and my other sister-in-law for all of their guidance and support in letting me cook many meals for them and their families.

Last but not least, a very big thank you to Marisa who spent countless hours fine-tuning and coming-up with great ideas regarding the cookbook.

To all my friends and my wonderful neighbor Linda McLean "a sister from another mother", thank you for supporting me and giving me the encouragement to get this cookbook off the ground. You have all allowed me to cook in my kitchen and yours to test my recipes with you and your families.

Nobody has been more important to me than my husband Greg of 25 years. He is my best friend, my soul mate, and my rock. He is my one true love and I want to thank him for all of his support. A special acknowledgement goes to my three children Gregory, Andrew, and Katrina. They are the love and the joy of my life! A big shout out goes to Katrina for her talents in help making the title cover. My kids are my motivation, inspiration, and encouragement to keep writing my Chomp College Cookbook. Their phone calls from college saying, "Mom we miss your cooking" is what made this cookbook happen.

You all have allowed me to explore and be creative with writing this cookbook. For that, I hold all my family, friends, and especially Tammy, in a special place in my heart.

Lastly, I would like to thank you, the readers, for taking the time to read this cookbook. I hope it gives you a helping hand in the kitchen teaching you how to make quick, healthy, and tasty recipes while juggling your busy college schedule.

Enjoy!

Made in the USA
Middletown, DE
26 September 2020